But God

Donna L. Francek Ternes

ISBN 979-8-88540-066-4 (paperback)
ISBN 979-8-88540-082-4 (hardcover)
ISBN 979-8-88540-067-1 (digital)

Christian Faith Publishing
832 Park Avenue
Meadville, PA 16335
www.christianfaithpublishing.com

Names have been changed to protect the privacy of the individuals.

Printed in the United States of America

I invite you on a journey—a devastatingly true story—of fear, pain, heartache, and sheer desperation. But in light of unfortunate events, God's overwhelming love and grace shined through. I pray it will encourage you and offer strength and hope even when circumstances may seem hopeless, and everything is crumbling. As a mother, what my daughter experienced affected me in ways I could never imagine.

To Abba Father
My beautiful daughter Sara Lynn

Sara A. and Sarah McPharlin
When we all get to heaven, what a day of rejoicing it will be!

Photo painted by Sara Lynn

But God...

I woke up that Saturday morning on December 15, 2018, not fully awake. I turned on my cell phone like I usually do when I get up. Unexpectedly, it rang instantly—the words "St. Johns" jumped off the screen. It was a hospital in the city. A terrible knot instantly grabbed my stomach. My only daughter, Sara, had not come home last night after going out to dinner with a friend. My gut told me that this particular phone call would be different. I had this dreadful feeling that this message was not good, and from this moment forward, my life was about to change forever.

The woman on the other end spoke with urgent words, stating that I should get to the hospital as quickly as possible. She could not give me any details over the phone. Immediately, I thought, *Was Sara in a fatal accident?* I fought intensely to push it out of my mind. As I rushed to wake up my husband, I told him we had to leave immediately for the hospital, which was an hour away from our home.

The Early Years

It was a cold spring day in 1984. I was scheduled for my first ultrasound scan and was approximately four months along in my first pregnancy. Upon my arrival, the technician directed me to the exam table where a complex machine stood nearby with a large screen. As I lay on the table, my eyes were fixated on the monitor. It revealed a shadowy image of a baby, perfectly developed. Her little heart was beating so rapidly. It looked as if it were outside her chest. At that precise moment, I felt a tiny foot kick me—as if she was letting me know that I was invading her quiet peaceful world. I giggled with delight as I witnessed the awe and wonder of this small life growing inside of me. I was not able to receive a photograph of her, but it did not matter because that image will be encrypted in my memory forever. I truly was head over heels in love with my baby.

As the months passed, my delivery date was rapidly approaching. It was late summer—a cool, bright, and crisp morning on September 18, 1984. I woke up not feeling well, a little nauseous. I was looking forward to my weekly checkup that afternoon. I thought to myself, *Today, this baby will be born.* When I arrived, I exuberantly said to my doctor, "I'm going to have this baby soon." Sure enough, I was in early labor and five hours later gave birth to a six-pound–fifteen-ounce little girl with dark hair.

All the nurses in the maternity ward were eager to tend to my new baby, and they commented on how beautiful she was. I vividly remember them saying they wanted to keep her with them. My response was, "No way. This is my baby." After a couple of days, I was ready to go home with my new bundle of joy and show her off to the world—but I became worried when the doctor told me she was jaundiced. The levels were dangerously elevated and needed to be brought down quickly, or she could develop brain damage. He ordered she be placed under a special light. It troubled me that she was subjected daily with needle pricks to test her blood, but thankfully after a few days, the danger passed, and we were able to go home.

Eventually, my family and friends stopped by to see her. They commented what a content and beautiful baby she was. She wasn't fussy and did not cry a lot. I possessed very strong maternal instincts and was completely relaxed and confident. I was elated in being a new mother.

When she was four months old, much to my surprise, I was expecting another child. I held unto my daughter and cried, overwhelmed at the thought of having two babies to take care of. As the days went by, I accepted the fact that another little person would be joining our family. Eight months later, just before Halloween, her brother Marty was born. She was so inquisitive around him—always touching, hugging, and kissing this stranger who seemed so tiny in comparison to how rapidly she was growing.

Interestingly, my babies' childhood illnesses always coincided with each other, like chicken pox and croup. It was similar to having twins. As their stages of development progressed, I remember Sara helping her little brother learn how to walk. Oh, how I cherish that image and keep it locked away in a very special place in my heart.

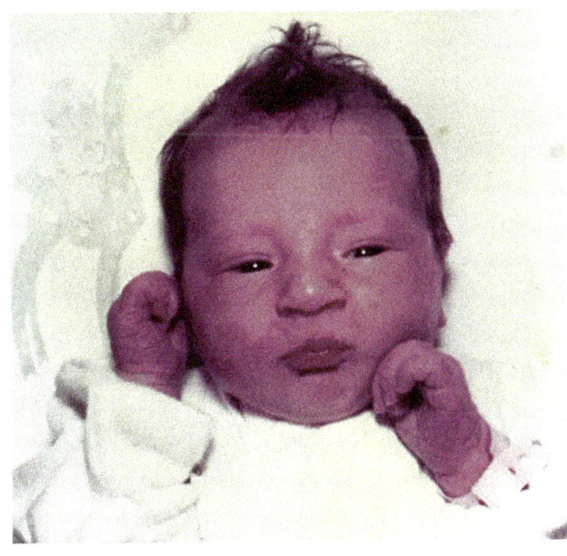

Up to the present time, we had lived in town. My husband and I decided that it was not a desirable place to raise our children, so the search was on for a country house. One summer afternoon, my toddlers and I went with my sister-in-law cruising down the country roads. Much to my delight, we approached an old farmhouse that desperately needed painting. Someone might even describe it as junky-looking. There was also a dilapidated barn, a silo, and some other old buildings on the property. But I was intrigued, so we turned slowly into the driveway, parked the car, and began walking around.

The grass was so tall; it came up to my knees and towered over my excited children. We made our way to the back of the house, and my sister-in-law found that the door was unlocked, so we walked inside. We had so much fun exploring this old neglected house, going from room to room. There was an outdated dingy carpet in the living room, but the first thought that came to my mind was, *I wonder if there is original hardwood underneath.* There was also a fireplace that had a family of raccoons living in it because of the *evidence* they left behind. Despite the work that would need to be done, I was eager to roll up my sleeves and make it a cozy home. I had this vision in my mind of a picturesque farmhouse surrounded by beautiful trees and flowers and a barn full of animals.

Shortly after, we located the farmers who owned the house, and we began renting. Two years later, we made the decision to purchase it. But much to my disappointment, the barn and the silo had to be torn down because of safety reasons. Fortunately, there was a chicken coop that served as a mini barn that housed all of our animals: ducks, rabbits, chickens, two turkeys, and years later, a couple of hogs and two goats named Ditty and Comet.

As Sara and Marty grew, they loved playing on our two acres. Our farmhouse was surrounded by fields of open land and woods nearby to explore and even a small country airport a distance down the road. There were cornfields to play hide-and-seek in and a big ditch that was filled with all manner of wildlife and frogs. Living in the country was fun, stimulating, and fulfilling, and there were endless discoveries to be made. We would go on "treasure hunts" in the woods and found a huge pile of cans and bottles that the farmers had dumped many years ago. It was so fun digging and searching for different shapes and colors. Sara enjoyed living in the country, and she developed a passionate love for animals.

When she turned five, her second brother, Andrew, was born, and I was adjusting to her going to school. It was a sad day for me when she rode on the school bus for the first time. I wasn't ready to let my firstborn go out into the world, gone from my watchful eyes. The first five years of her life went by so quickly—in a blink of an eye. Through second grade, Sara had attended public school. When she entered the third grade, I chose to homeschool my children, but after six months, I decided to send them back to public school. I found out the hard way. They had a difficult time sticking to the lessons, and I was asking myself if the material presented was adequate.

In the meantime, the seasons were rolling along. In the summers, her dad would cut trails in the nearby field, and we would take walks with our dogs and pick clover. Sara was certain there was a four-leafed one out there somewhere. I relish those rare times we had together as a family. In our front yard, there were two giant willow trees with a low spot that would hold water and freeze in the winter. Sara would go ice-skating under them, and she was becoming quite good at it.

Another family event we always did together in early summer was picking giant sweet strawberries at the berry farm. Sara would always eat more than she picked. One of our favorite breakfast items was french toast made with our own fresh duck eggs with sliced strawberries on them. Every spring, I planted a garden. The kids would munch on fresh green beans, potatoes, tomatoes, and cantaloupes. At the end of summer, I would be busy canning tomatoes and processing our poultry. I loved having the freezer full of fresh meat for my family to enjoy during the long cold Michigan winters.

Furthermore, we were fortunate to live close to Lake Huron. On hot summer days, we would hop in the car and head to the beach and have picnics. Sara absolutely loved the water—I'm pretty sure fish DNA flowed in her blood. She was always the first one to rush into the waves and search for pretty rocks and shiny beach glass along the glistening shoreline.

Sara, having loved animals, had an obsession at a young age—baby kittens. Stray cats would frequently show up on our large front porch. Once, a pretty calico cat arrived with a very "plump" belly. Days later, a litter of the cutest kittens were born in our back room. Another prominent memory I have was when we were driving down the country road, and we spotted two kittens in the ditch. We immediately stopped, and Sara and Marty jumped out of the car. They scooped them up, squealing, "Mom, can we keep 'em, please?"

I couldn't refuse, and Leo and Lenny came home to live with us.

Many years later as a teenager, Sara would wander across the street to the neighbor's farm. She brought home a tiny female kitten that was scratching and hissing—It didn't take long to tame that bundle of fur—she named her Puddy.

As mentioned earlier, there was a small airport just down the road from our house. We had the rare chance to ride in a four-seater airplane. I recall all of us squeezing in the back seat—the kids were bubbling with excitement. We flew over our small town and along the Lake Huron shoreline. It was mesmerizing looking at everything below us: the tiny farmhouses, the patterns of the farmer's fields, algae-filled ponds, and the trees. It was a different world up there. Although Sara was young, she never forgot it.

One day when she was seven years old, Sara asked if we could get some candy at the store, which was two miles away from our house. Her dad and I had told her, "No, we cannot go today."

It was a Saturday afternoon, and we were cleaning up the yard. She and her brothers were outside playing. During this time, we noticed she was not around. We searched frantically everywhere for her—it seemed she had just vanished in thin air.

Terrified something bad had happened to her, we called the police. Some time had gone by, and she finally returned on her own. She admitted to stealing a quarter from her dad and walked to town by herself. We talked to her about her actions and how she had deliberately disobeyed us. Thank God, this never happened again.

Another incident occurred that same year—she was relentless in asking to get a home permanent. I eventually gave in and allowed her to get one. She soon regretted it because the perm solution was uncomfortable. After that, she never got a perm again.

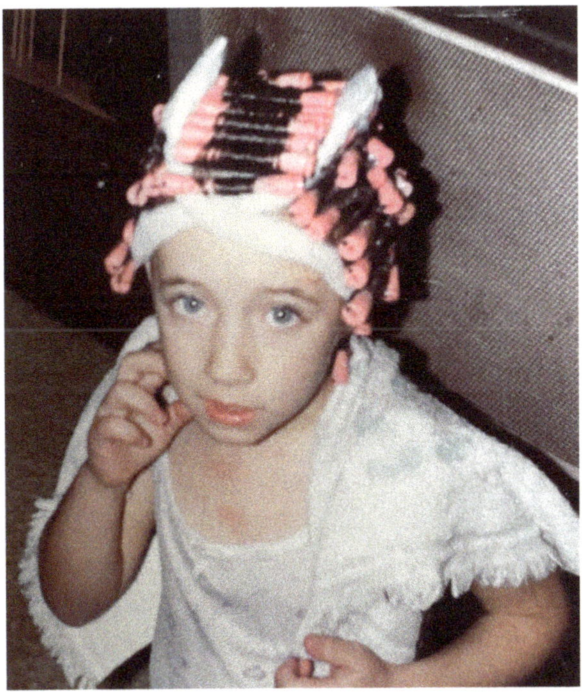

Not long after, I realized that my children were getting older and needed spiritual influence in their lives. We regularly visited a small nondenominational church and became very involved for about seven years. At the age of eight, Sara asked Jesus in her heart. Although she enjoyed church very much, occasionally on a Sunday, she would fake not feeling well. Unfortunately for her, the sick act never worked as I was firm in my children's church attendance.

Sara's childhood, for the most part, was like many of us who grew up in Michigan. We enjoyed summer carnivals, 4-H fairs, going swimming at the beach, and ice-skating in the winter. In addition, it was a big occasion when anyone in the family had a birthday. All the cousins would gather together and have cake, ice cream, and lots of fun. I always made sure my children visited their grandparents' farm on the weekends. It was important to me to have a close relationship with them. During the holidays, it was a tradition when family members would gather around "the mile-long wooden dining table" and devour homemade tasty meals.

Finally, one of the best times we had was in the summer of 1999. We took our only family vacation to Geauga Lake in Ohio. Sara was ecstatic riding the wooden rollercoaster—and in sharp contrast—her brother Marty and I were terrified and hung on for dear life! It was exhilarating watching dolphins jumping through hoops and doing tricks. The best part, though, was when we were able to pet one—I remember it felt just like a wet watermelon.

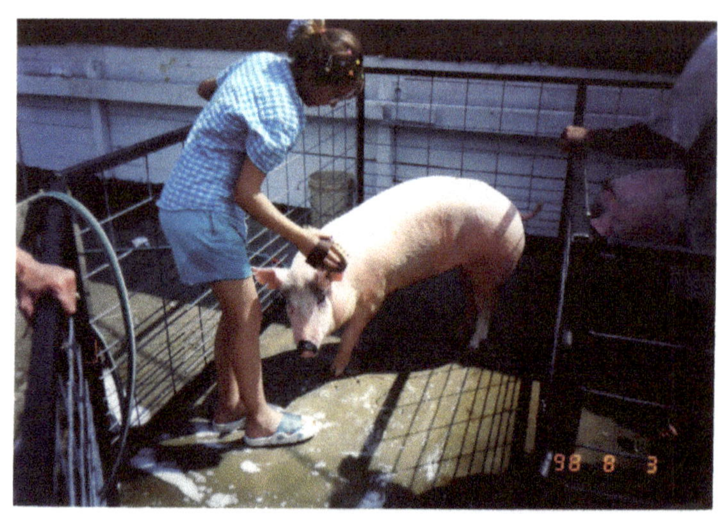

Growing Pains

In Sara's thirteenth year, one day we had gone shopping. Because we lived a good thirty minutes away from a large store, it wasn't something we did often. She had asked me if I could buy her some makeup. I explained that we didn't have any extra money. Abruptly in a huff, she walked away upset. Without my knowledge, she shoplifted some makeup and was caught by a store associate. We were both directed to go to the manager's office. Thankfully, the manager was gracious and did not press charges. I was so embarrassed and had to pay a fine of $100.

Another year went by, and I received a phone call from the school. She had fallen and hurt her wrist. I rushed her to the hospital because it was severely swollen, and she was in excruciating pain. They took x-rays and determined she had broken it and had to wear a cast for six weeks. After it healed, Sara got her first job at the local A&W restaurant. She was so excited to earn money and buy whatever she wanted. Expensive taste was in her blood, and having designer shoes and clothing to wear was important to her. And I felt it was good that she learned the responsibility of money management.

The next Spring in early March, there had not been much rain, and everything was parched. The fields that surrounded our house had old dry grass from the previous year with about a hundred acres of newly planted pine trees. As I walked by the window in the house, I saw smoke coming from our backyard. I shouted, "The field is on fire!"

We grabbed shovels and struggled in vain to put out the flames. The neighbors called the local fire department. I could hear the siren blaring in the distance. It was like having a horrible nightmare. I was standing in the middle of the field, utterly exhausted. The sky above me was swirling with smoke, and blackened soil was beneath my feet. I started crying. I was so grateful that the fire had not spread to buildings or nearby houses. Later that day, Sara admitted to playing with matches. We were mandated by the fire chief to pay a hefty fine. Thirty acres had been burned that terrible day along with hundreds of pine trees. I was so angry with her and thought to myself, *Why would my daughter play with matches? She certainly knows right from wrong.*

In conclusion, around the age of sixteen, she experienced her first love. He was also a teenager, and Sara became a frequent visitor at his house. They would play video games, and she would paint with his mother. She was a positive influence on Sara, helping her tap into a hidden talent no one knew she possessed. As a result, her painting ability was blossoming, and she was the top student in her art class in high school. As time wore on though, they stopped hanging out together and went their separate ways. Years later, she told me this was when she experimented with cigarettes, marijuana, and lost her virginity.

Sadly, not long after, her dad and I also went our separate ways and got a divorce due to irreconcilable differences. During one of our rare talks, Sara told me, "It was like a dam burst inside her, and she just lost control." I have a lot of regrets about not spending extra time with my children during this difficult time.

Later, Sara graduated from high school. She began working at another restaurant as a waitress and then at a pet store. She even enrolled in a couple of college courses. Her goal at the time was to save money and buy her first car. Well, she did purchase one—she promised to make monthly payments if I would be her cosigner. I was happy for her, but the way she drove made me extremely nervous.

Furthermore, it wasn't long before she fell in love again—with a young man who was from Tennessee, working in Michigan. One day out of the blue, she said, "Mom, I'm packing up my stuff and Puddy and driving to Tennessee. You know how I've always wanted to go there."

After staying down there a couple of months, she started a job at a steakhouse. In fact, she made a couple of new friends. Becky, her coworker, asked her parents if Sara could stay with them until she found a place to live. Her other friend, Danny, was a great guy, and they immediately all became good friends. But all of this was unsettling for me because she was hundreds of miles away.

Eventually, she called me and said she and her boyfriend broke up. She also smashed her car and wanted to come home. So my fiancé and I got into his van and drove to Tennessee and brought her and Puddy home.

In the autumn of 2005, I had two major life events. First, I married my fiancé. I was looking forward to spending the rest of my life with this man. Secondly, my sister called me on the morning of Halloween and told me that our only brother had died. I was numb with grief. He had struggled many years with drugs and alcohol and died from a fentanyl overdose. He was only thirty-six years old.

At the age of twenty, Sara started another job as a waitress. A new relationship soon blossomed between her and the manager. They were with each other all the time and would go out with friends and hang out. I was appalled they were engaging in drug usage, alcohol, and having sex. Also, this was when she began taking an antidepressant and had overdosed. I was disappointed and troubled. I thought, *Where did I go wrong?*

Meanwhile, Sara had accumulated credit card debt that went beyond her means of payment. My new husband and I hired a lawyer for her, and she filed for bankruptcy. We bailed her out. Looking back in retrospect, "Should we have done that?"

Hence, I had been praying that God would get her attention and help her to make better choices. I was getting increasingly alarmed about her future. We started getting into arguments about her decisions and were growing further and further apart.

As a parent, I always had high hopes for a bright future for Sara. She had connected with her old boyfriend, who was working for a traveling entertainment company. He said they were hiring, and he could get her a job. I remember her being so excited about this opportunity as she loved to travel. We bought her the plane ticket to Houston, Texas, where she would go through the hiring process. Maybe her life would get back on track, and the things that had been holding her back were a thing of the past.

Unfortunately, what was supposed to be a new start for her ended up disastrous. One morning, a coworker found her in bed, and she couldn't get up. She had taken the drug ecstasy. I was shocked and wondered, *Where in the world did she get that from?* I cannot describe my feelings. Let me just say—hopelessness was seeping deep into my being. It seemed that whenever I would get a speck of hope, things would fall apart. She would make good progress, then "BAM!" something would happen and send her right back to square one. What could I do? Today's society states that she is an adult, capable of making her own decisions. Where do you get the help you so desperately need when a person is consistently wreaking havoc on their family and on themselves?

Now that Sara was an adult, her impetuous decisions caused more harm—mentally, emotionally, physically, financially, and spiritually. Her erratic behaviors were becoming more frequent. Episodes of crying, extreme impulsiveness, and moodiness were almost an everyday occurrence for her. It was as if something had taken possession of her—like she had another personality. My daughter was becoming someone I didn't know.

In the summer of 2009, at the age of twenty-five, she was admitted for her first psychiatric admission into a mental health unit. After a series of tests, the doctor diagnosed that Sara had bipolar disorder, borderline personality disorder, fibromyalgia, and depression. This caused her to be on several medications, and eventually, she would abuse the doctor's recommendations and take more than the prescription called for. She reached out for mental health services, but even with all the help she was receiving, the unpredictable behavior continued and was becoming progressively worse.

Darkness Settles In

For many long, seemingly endless years, I was on this emotional roller-coaster with my daughter. One day, she would be fine and say, "I love you, Mom." The next day, she would be mean and couldn't stand me. I was bewildered what would make her *flip* like a light switch. Needless to say, it was exhausting and difficult to endure. It seemed trying to please her was impossible. There was constant tension between us. It would get to where I couldn't take it anymore and would have to get away from her. There was absolutely no way I could live with her in the same house, or I'm sure I would have lost my sanity.

Unfortunately, Sara was very rebellious and had a lot of trouble getting along with my family. She would lie, manipulate, and steal from them. Needless to say, no one trusted her and avoided her. Sadly, she and her dad did not get along either. They had an extremely rocky relationship. Over the years, she would move in with him and then move out because she had nowhere else to go.

Because she was very headstrong and had no self-control, she would shoplift and then get caught. I cannot recall exactly how many times she went to jail for retail fraud—I'm guessing about eight times. Lawlessness was quickly becoming her way of life. Breaking and entering, larceny, operating a car while under the influence of drugs, and possession of marijuana were on her list of convictions. Her friends were drug addicts, and they were constantly getting into trouble, having no regard for anything except getting their next fix. They reminded me of animals who were out of control. I always dreaded when she called me because it usually meant that she needed money or a place to stay. I didn't know my own child anymore—she was like a stranger to me.

As a mother, I should be able to protect and nurture my child, an instinct ordained by God. I felt so helpless and miserable at times. I would think to myself, *Why can't Sara just be normal? Why can't we have a close relationship like other moms and their daughters?* Sometimes when I was shopping, I would see other mothers with their daughters, laughing and smiling. I would look away and sigh deeply and fight back tears.

So many nights, I would cry and beg God to watch over and protect her. There would be periods of time I would not see or hear from her for months at a time. I never knew where she was, who she was with, or what trouble was she getting into. I recall a time when I didn't have any contact with her for six months. When I finally saw her, she was covered with a red itchy rash. I said, "Sara you need to go to a doctor and have that looked at."

She had unknowingly contracted scabies. At the time she was living in a car, with her mentally deranged boyfriend Joe. This was an extremely toxic relationship. He would repeatedly rape her and give her heroin. There was an incident when they were driving down the freeway and arguing. He was so cruel. He pushed her out of his van. The only thing Sara told me about that terrifying event was that she got a hairline skull fracture. This was one of the worst times in her life, and I probably don't know half of it. A memory that just now struck me is when she told me, "Mom, you have no idea the drugs that I've taken. I should have been dead a long time ago."

Joe, unfortunately, was renting a second-story apartment in a two-story house, not far away from our home. It had a porch with a sloped roof. One incident that is clear in my mind. One night she was so drugged up, she jumped out onto the roof, then down onto his van that was parked below. I got a phone call from her. She was crying, saying she needed to go to the emergency room because she broke her feet. We picked her up, and the hospital staff took an x-ray. Thankfully, nothing was broken.

She hobbled out of the hospital that night really mad at me, but I don't remember the reason. It was a miracle she was still alive after being with this vile man. I was so relieved when she finally got away from him after about a year. Unfortunately, her addiction to drugs did not go away. I watched in horror—as my daughter's life was slipping away into a deep, dark abyss—and I feared for her very life. I could do nothing but pray for her and ask God to intervene and save her from certain destruction.

I'm going to share a prayer that I wrote to God.

> Lord, you already know what I'm going to say. Sara has some major drug problems. If you don't step in, then I'm afraid I will lose her. Your Word says that you will not give me more than I can handle. I don't know if I could handle losing Sara to death. I've already lost my only brother to death from drugs. Lord, if my prayers can change her destiny, I will praise you forever. I pray that these heartfelt words are not in vain.
>
> Also, your Word says to cast all my cares on you because you care for me. Help me to cast my worries to you, Lord. Somehow, some way, change her destiny. Turn around what the devil means for evil to good. Jesus, help Sara to resist the devil and run far away from him. Cause the scales to fall from her eyes so that she can see the truth. Save her from herself, her own self-destructiveness. Remove the people in her life that influence her to make wrong choices. Cause her to remember your Word.
>
> Your Word is the most powerful force on earth. By your Word, you made the heavens and the earth. Your Word will not return void but will accomplish the very thing that it was sent to do. My heart is broken over Sara's choices. Only you can change her heart, soften her heart. Thank you for hearing my prayers. Thank you for who you are and what you are going to do in the future, amen.

I learned a decade later that God doesn't always answer our prayers the way we think He should.

Grasping at Straws

In the month of April 2010, I became a grandmother for the first time. My oldest son and his wife had a beautiful baby girl. I was thrilled! But dark menacing clouds would soon overshadow my happiness as Sara's life was spiraling wildly out of control. Something drastic needed to be done to get her some help. A friend from my teenage years generously agreed to take her into his home. I was so grateful and relieved she wasn't living on the streets or in a car.

I was so desperate to get her some help. I went to my pastor at the church we were attending. They told us about a Christian rehabilitation center in Pennsylvania. After researching it, I talked to Sara, and she agreed to go—even though she was hesitant. This program was thirteen months in length. It was my greatest hope that she would learn coping skills and self-control, love herself, and develop healthy habits. Specifically, she would have a personal counselor, attend life skill classes, go to church, and attend Bible studies.

My friend agreed to drive us, and we prepared for the long drive. We had to go clothes shopping because Sara didn't have a proper wardrobe. I had made reservations ahead of time for a hotel that was in close proximity to the rehabilitation center. I planned on getting a few hours of rest before we admitted her. I was eager to be there the first thing in the morning and not give her any chance of changing her mind. On the way there, she had been crying, saying, "I don't know if I can do this for thirteen months."

By then, we were halfway there—there was no turning back. That trip took nine hours. We arrived at the hotel at three thirty in the morning. I was exhausted and slipped into the bed. It was so hard for me to relax, but I finally dozed off for a few hours.

At 8:00 a.m., I woke up and told Sara to get up and get ready. She grumbled and rustled around in the bed, not budging. I said, "Come on it's time to get up. You have to be there by 9:00 a.m." I walked across the hall and woke up my friend. I told him she didn't want to get up.

He stormed into our room and yelled at her, "If you don't get up, we are leaving you here." Sara's strong self-will was in high gear.

True to his word, he said to me, "Come on. Let's go." I had to call the rehab center and tell them she refused to go. This was on Good Friday, and even though the building was closed, they agreed to take her. But there was nothing they could do—she had to admit herself.

We left her at the hotel and drove back to Michigan. I was really hoping she would change her mind and go. I remember as we drove away, I was sobbing bitterly about leaving her there all alone. I was so disappointed, heartbroken, and angry. Why wouldn't she just go?

When I finally arrived back home, my husband informed me Sara's former depraved boyfriend Joe called him. Somehow, he found out she was left at the hotel. He wanted my husband to give him his credit card information for the room. My husband was wise and did not comply, so she was kicked out of the hotel.

Later, she met a woman who gave her a place to stay. Two weeks after that, my friend drove to Toledo, Ohio, and picked her up. He dropped her off at her dad's house. However, this didn't last too long because they would start fighting again.

Sooner or later, I knew Sara would show up at my house. Sure enough, one morning at 1:00 a.m., she knocked at my door. I had just gone to bed a few hours earlier because I had to get up early the next morning for work. She begged me to let her stay one night and ended up sleeping for three days. I had no idea she was going through heroin withdrawals. I had not seen her or heard from her for some time.

When she was rested, she became demanding, argumentative, and disrespectful. When I was at work, she would snoop through my personal belongings and steal items. I hid the medication that she was taking because she took too many. I flushed them down the toilet.

Talking about her pills was always challenging and frustrating. She was obsessed with them and would get very defensive and make up excuses why she had to take more than what the doctor prescribed.

It took every ounce of strength I had to not want to strike her. She would push me to the limits constantly. I often wondered how I could love and loathe her at the same time.

I prayed, "Please, Lord, direct and protect Sara. You know she is my only daughter. Please don't let anything happen to her. Please protect her from harm and evil. Help me to release her to you and to trust you with her. You love her so much more than I ever could. Help me to not be anxious for anything. My petition to you today is to save my daughter from death and self-destruction. Help her to help herself. Help me to be a good mother to her. Thank you, Jesus! Amen."

I need to pause here for a moment—I am sitting at my desk, surrounded by journals, court documents, letters, and cards from Sara. I really don't know why I've kept them. Possibly as mementos to share with her when she got better so she could look back and see the progress she made.

There have been days that I haven't wanted to write at all. It's too painful, and I just want to forget these awful memories and bury them deep. Her life reminds me of the movie *Jumanji* where they uncover the mysterious game that wreaks havoc on anyone who happens to play it. It gets *buried* so it doesn't return to the surface and cause massive destruction again. Oh, how I wish I could bury this life my daughter was living and start a new one, a happy and fruitful one—but unfortunately, I'm not permitted to tamper with fate.

Grim Reality

My husband and I left that December morning, not knowing anything about Sara's condition. On the drive to the hospital, I silently prayed, "Jesus, give me the strength to handle whatever it is that I will have to face today." Instantly, this picture flashed in my mind of her lying in a hospital bed, tubes, and a machine hooked up to her body with beams of reflecting sunlight shining through the window of her room.

When we arrived, we were directed to go to the ICU unit. It was a secured area that required permission to be let in by the staff. We followed our way around the long hallway, and there she was—exactly as the picture I saw in my mind. It was kind of weird because I didn't break down sobbing. I went to her bedside, took her hand, and kissed her forehead. I said, "I'm here, Sara. It's Mom."

I felt a calmness—as if I was enveloped by an invisible cushion. The nurse attending to her care said Sara had arrived by ambulance the night before. She went on to say that she had gone over thirty minutes without oxygen, causing her brain to swell. Therefore, she had to be put on life support. I recall her words, "It doesn't look good." The course of treatment was to lower her body temperature to ninety-two degrees to see if this would relieve the pressure. I remember touching Sara and thinking, *Wow, she feels really cold.*

The nurse called in the neurosurgeon, and he stated, "The next forty-eight to seventy-two hours are crucial." So the waiting, hoping, and praying began—for five very long days.

World of Chaos

For three years, Sara had been in and out of jail for shoplifting. I was looking through her belongings recently and found a letter that I had written to her in December of 2011. Here is what I said:

> Sara, the spirit of God works within you to transform you into His image, but you must do your part. Your job is to respond to the work being done inside you. You must relinquish all sin, build up your spirit by reading God's Word, open your heart to wisdom and counsel, and surrender your old nature to be replaced by your new one. Your spiritual growth is intended to be a collaboration between you and God (meaning He will work with you).
>
> This process is often difficult, but it brings great rewards. He wants to hear from your heart. He wants sincerity. He wants honesty. For a humble and contrite heart, He will not turn away from. Ask and it shall be given to you. Ask with the right motives. Draw closer to God, and He will draw closer to you. Sara, when you look for Him with your whole heart, you will find Him. When you earnestly and desperately look for Him, you will find Him.
>
> Begin reading the book of John in the New Testament. Seek Him continually, and He will meet with you. He will reveal Himself to you when He knows you really mean business and

are not just playing games. For He knows your motives and your heart. He will examine your heart to see if you are really serious about wanting Him. Thank Him, praise Him, bow down to Him, worship Him, pray to Him.

I guarantee you will find what you need in Him. Ask Him to give you the motivation and the desire and the hunger to want to know Him, to want to seek Him. Ask Him to help you love Him.

There are things every day in your life that will pull you away from Him. It is a matter of spiritual life or spiritual death. You choose. Which do you want? Life or death? It's up to you to pursue and maintain a relationship with your creator. He will not push Himself on you. He is always waiting on you to come to Him. So GO and don't STOP!

Love,
Mom

Furthermore, because of her health issues, Sara qualified for social security disability. She had such a difficult time using those finances for productive things, like a roof over her head. Her priorities were having enough cigarettes, pills, and of course—drugs. I was too frustrated and overwhelmed trying to help her because she was so disagreeable, and we constantly argued about me handling her money. I petitioned the court to appoint a legal guardian for her, due to her inability to handle money and maintain a stable living environment for herself. I felt a guardian was crucial for her well-being, not to mention alleviated a lot of stress in my life.

Eventually, Sara would be hospitalized eight times in a year—for attempted suicide. I was so exasperated, I can't believe I didn't lose my mind. I thank God for that guardian. She decided that Sara might benefit from living in an adult foster care home. At least she would be supervised, have a roof over her head, and hopefully stay out of trouble. However, she opposed the rules and stayed up all night, disrupting the whole house. She was eventually evicted. In addition, although the year is foggy in my memory—she was at a halfway house—but again being in another home with other people did not work out. Finally, the guardian arranged for Sara to get her own apartment. She was able to get Puddy and settle in—for about a year. I was so excited and purchased some dishes and a microwave for her new place. I was certain this was going to work this time.

Meanwhile, I told Sara about a church that was located near her apartment. I was delighted she started attending the services and learning about God. It was my hope that she would surrender her life to Him completely. I was feeling that the darkness was finally starting to dissipate in her life. The pastor and his wife took Sara under their wings. They told me she was like one of their own kids. If she was having an unusually difficult time, they would go to her apartment and pray with her.

On occasion, I would meet with them, and together we all laid hands on her and prayed. She seemed to be heading on a good path and even got baptized. All that was taking place in her life at that time was special to me. The memories I have will linger forever in my heart. I will always be grateful to the pastor and his wife for their kindness, love, and time they spent with my daughter.

With a grateful heart, I prayed, "Abba Father, I really want to thank you for all you are doing in Sara's life. Father, you know her heart. Please draw near to her, give her a strong desire to please you, read your Word and to do what it says. Holy Spirit, permeate her entire being. Reach deep into her soul and give her godly wisdom and discernment. When she is around other people who are not good, give her the strength to run from them! Cause her to close her eyes to evil. Cause her to embrace Christ and all that He is. Cause her to fall head over heels in love with Jesus and never be satisfied with anyone or anything else. Cause her to be the woman of God that you created her to be. Father God, thank you for loving Sara so much that you died for her. Thank you for setting her feet upon the "Rock," Jesus, her Lord and Savior. Amen!"

However, even though I was hopeful she was making progress, she was still getting into trouble. It was very distressing for me.

One incident that is clear in my memory was a time she had just shoplifted from my friend's store. She ran off but showed up sometime later at my doorstep. I was forced to call the police and have her taken to jail. It was absolutely heart-wrenching watching the car drive away. My heart ached so badly. No words can describe how a mother feels when she has no choice but to turn her child over to the law. It leaves you feeling physically sick, not to mention wanting to scream at the top of your lungs.

I remember mentioning to a few people—someday I should write a book about this—no one would ever believe her life—it's like a crazy soap opera. It makes *Days of Our Lives* look like *Sesame Street*. I wrote in my journal, "Please, Lord, give me strength and wisdom on how to handle this chaos in my life. I don't know what to do anymore. Sara is continuing down this destructive path. She is destroying her life every day. She is suffering, and I can't seem to help her."

He then led me to this comforting scripture: "Why am I discouraged? Why is my heart so sad? I will put my hope in God! I will praise him again—my savior and my God" (Psalm 42:5–6 NLT)! I hung onto those precious words for a very long time as they gave me immense comfort and peace.

So here is a letter Sara sent me concerning her guardian.

> Mom, in my own defense, I need to get rid of this guardian. I want to handle my own affairs and learn to live on my own—completely. Do you have even the slightest clue how it feels to have to ask a woman who is fake and doesn't communicate properly at all *for my own money?* I want to get out of this dried-up hick town. I prosper in prosperous places. I want to get rid of Maggie and that apartment. This would be huge for me, my self-esteem, and give me a greater sense of responsibility by knowing I don't have a safety net. I want to be 100 percent in charge of my

bills, my health, my everything. Am I making sense? This will create a challenge for me. I have discovered that I thrive on challenges. Positive challenges will produce positive results. I tend to create challenges for myself when I am bored. When I am in a negative frame of mind, I create negative challenges. What I'm getting at is being fully in charge of every single aspect of my life. With an income, it should and will, keep me busy enough to stay out of trouble. You know, Mom, I did great when I was in college and was working. Please take this letter seriously. Please take this to the judge and release me from this guardian. Please try and step in my shoes concerning my independence. Love you, Mom.

Sara

By the same token, If I tried to talk to her about being on her own, without her guardian's direction, the arguments would begin. She would get mad at me and say mean things like, "What a terrible mother you are" and "You really don't care about me." Then the vicious cycle of not speaking to each other would occur, sometimes for months at a time. There were countless times that I just wanted to walk away and turn my back on her.

Undoubtedly, the poor guardian was run ragged for three years. One time she arranged for Sara to enter a detox center. That morning, she went to pick her up at her apartment, but Sara refused to comply and wouldn't answer the door. The police were finally called to make sure she was okay. I was so disgusted. The guardian had wasted her time trying to get help for her but to no avail.

I cried out to God, "I refuse to give in to despair, defeat, and depression. I am not defined by others, especially by Sara. The enemy is relentless in trying to use her against me. So let all that I am praise the Lord! I have value in Christ and HIM ALONE! I am who HE SAYS I AM! I shut the lies and false accusations of the devil from my mind and my heart. She really is out to hurt me and make my life miserable. I've blocked her number from my phone. I just can't take this anymore.

"When I don't give her what she wants, it's like World War III. I do not have to subject myself to her abusiveness and sheer cruelty. I don't have to do anything for her. So, God, I've hardened my heart against her. I don't want to be around her, see her, hear her lies and manipulations anymore. She is a very ill person, and I cannot do this anymore. One day, she is hysterical making suicidal threats, and the next day sweet as can be.

"I've heard it so many times, God! It is so crazy and ridiculous! How can anyone live like that? I can't, and I won't! I refuse! I won't go through this torment ANYMORE!"

Sometimes, we have to calcify our feelings to protect our hearts from continuous injury.

Unstable Winds

Finally, Sara got what she wanted. She packed her bags, dropped off Puddy at her dad's, and took a bus to Colorado Springs. The guardian had no idea that she even left—until I called her. Her chances of returning were slim to none, so the guardian petitioned the court, and the guardianship was terminated.

In August of 2014, I wrote,

> It is with a heavy heart I write today. Sara left last night for Colorado. She left mad at me because I didn't do something for her that she was responsible for. She told me she was never going to see me again. My heart just aches to have a real relationship with her. I pray she has a safe trip and that your angels would protect her and guard her. Even though she treats me bad, I still love her.

The next evening, I received a call late at night. A police sergeant told me that Sara cut her legs on the bus with a knife and then voluntarily admitted herself to a psych hospital. I thought, *Why can't she just be normal?* Why does she always have to get into trouble wherever she goes? *What a horrible way to start a new beginning in a new state.*

After she got out of the psych hospital, she met a young lady and lived with her for six months. Sara phoned me, saying she was going to California. I knew she had worn out her welcome. I could not believe she had the guts to go that far away by herself. I thought, *She is really dumb or incredibly brave. I'm not sure which one.*

I knew once she made up her mind about something, it was virtually impossible to talk her out of it. So again, I asked the Lord to watch over her and protect her. I'm sure by now He was really tired of me asking for the same thing over and over.

Meanwhile, on the flight to California, she met a guy named Evan. Soon, they were chatting away as if they were old friends. Sara was sharing with him how she had always wanted to go out West and put her feet in the Pacific Ocean and smell the salty air. When she landed at her destination, she stayed in a hotel. She called me and wanted me to pay for additional days to stay there, but I told her no.

On the plane, she must have gotten Evan's number, so she called him. He agreed to let her stay with him. He had a job that required that he travel, so she had his whole house to herself. She spent that winter in sunny California. It was now 2015. She phoned me a few times, telling me that they went to the ocean, had fun at local attractions, and went shopping. He even took her to Hollywood. She was living the dream.

Before too long, though, trouble was brewing in paradise. She contacted me a few times crying, saying that he was into witchcraft, and they were fighting horribly with each other. The relationship was escalating into physical fights, and she got arrested. The sad thing was, I never really knew what was going on in her life. She was gone a whole year, but it seemed much longer to me. Quickly, the love and romance fizzled out in beautiful California, and it was time for her to move on. So she hopped on a plane and came back home to Michigan.

Now that Sara was back home, my husband and I did not want her staying with us because of her past behaviors, so we put her up in a nearby hotel for a week. At the end of that week, we wanted to pay for her to stay another week, but the management said, "No, she is causing too much of a disturbance here."

Once again, Sara was bouncing around looking for a place to stay. If she stayed at a family member's house, it always ended up in turmoil. She always wanted to run their house and did not respect their property. Everyone was absolutely fed up! Back to her dad's she would go. It was like mixing oil with water between them—the arguing would start, and she would leave—again.

Once Sara realized her back was against the wall, and she had nowhere to live, I asked her again about going to the rehab in Pennsylvania—the thirteen-month program. Her response was, "I will think about it." She finally agreed to go. By that time, it was August of 2015. So for the second time, we had to get proper clothes, new eyeglasses, and fix a tooth that was bothering her. Money had to be sent ahead of time so she would have a bed when she arrived.

I thought about the "last time" I had taken her to Pennsylvania. The emotional pain and frustration I went through made me shudder. This time, I asked a godly friend from our church, someone I trusted, to ride with my husband. Together, they agreed to make the long trip. I didn't want to go with them for fear Sara would back out again. I was so thankful to God. I fell on my knees on the kitchen floor, crying tears of gratitude, that this was finally going to happen— my daughter was going to get the help she so desperately needed.

I need to express, I'm doing my best, with God's help, in remembering all of these events that took place. Writing in my journals is what helped keep me sane. There were so many instances that happened with Sara—it's just not possible to recall every single one. I'm convinced when they happened, writing them out helped me to cope with all those emotions and feelings. Communicating on paper was very therapeutic for me, and it was a healthy way for me to release what I was experiencing, the positive and the negative.

I strongly suggest that if anyone is going through something unbearable right now—write it down—all of it—the good, the bad, and the ugly. It really does help to release those emotions. Finally, if you cannot afford to see a professional counselor, who better to pour your heart out to than God? He is great at listening. I am living proof that He does answer prayer—and best of all—He won't send you a bill.

When Sara FINALLY arrived in Pennsylvania and got settled in, she wrote me letters and *thank you* cards of how much she appreciated being there. The staff and her roommates were accommodating and pleasant. My hopes for her to stay in the program were at an all-time high. I felt this gigantic weight being lifted from me. I could "finally breathe" and smile. When anyone would ask me how is Sara doing, I was genuinely happy to report she was doing "fantastic."

In her very first letter from Pennsylvania, she wrote this to me.

> Mom, oh, my gosh! I love it here! There are only eight of us girls here. They liked me right away! Today was the church service. It was *so* awesome! The Holy Spirit just drips in the air. I'm protected here. Mom, thank you so frigging much! Like I wish I would have come here earlier, but God's timing prepping me is working. Oh, by the way, I'M STAYING UNTIL I GRADUATE! I'm going to finish this through. It's about time I do something all the way, and it couldn't be for a better reason. I AM GOING TO TRANSFORM. It's time to let out what's been locked inside. God is *so* GOOD! This is the best thing that ever happened to me—thanks to you. Thank you, Mom and John. I love you both so much! God Bless!
>
> Sara

Reading her letter was indescribable. My "DREAM" for my child has finally come true! Later, in another letter, she told me that in the first five weeks, she thought about leaving. She was attending the required classes and doing chores, going to church and Bible study, and talking to her counselor, but the enemy was really *battling* against her, multiple times a day. But she managed to retain control with God's help. She said she stood up in church one Sunday and gave her *testimony*, and everyone in the room stood up and clapped for her. The story she shared was "she was fighting for her life and to stay there and seek God."

She wrote to me: "I'm still here because of what God is doing through them." Finally, a third letter arrived, and I thought, *I hope she doesn't bail.* She wrote,

> Mom, you know it's really hard for me to stay in one place. If you came to see me, it would give me fuel and more determination to see this through.

I just experienced another rough patch about facing things about myself. I had so much anger and rage. I wanted to leave so bad, you have no idea. But, Mom, I'm working this through. This is a hard program, ask anyone here. I can't wait to see you. Keep praying for me.

Love,
Sara

However, as the weeks continued on—like hairline fractures in a foundation—things began to crack and crumble. The intensity of the program was forcing her to face herself and her negative behaviors, and she rebelled. The pressure was overwhelming for her, and she left the premises without permission and bought some cigarettes and got kicked out. There was money in her account for one bus ticket, and she took a bus back to Michigan. When she got to the station, she tried to call me, but I was working. When I was able to return her call, she pleaded with me to come and pick her up. I firmly replied, "No, Sara. I'm not picking you up." She called her counselor, and they agreed to give her one more chance. We purchased a bus ticket back to Pennsylvania.

When she returned, they explained to her that she would have to start over again with the program. That meant she would be there longer than the original thirteen months, and amazingly, she agreed. Here is a letter I received when she returned:

"Hey, Mom! So I've been back here for a few days. It feels so good to be back (home). The day I left, we had a spiritual growth class that the pastor taught. It was about the prodigal son. Let me tell you. I was hanging on the edge of my seat, knowing I was getting kicked out. How did he know I was coming back? God is so awesome! When you didn't show up at the bus station, and I couldn't reach you, I put my entire existence in God's hands. I got out my Bible and started reading it right in front of everyone, knowing that every breath I took depended on Him. Despite that I was devastated leaving here, my attitude toward this place has changed dramatically. I'm more serious about my well-being, about submitting—everything! I want to do everything right this time around. Since I've returned, everyone is telling me that there's a positive difference in how I'm behaving. My ability to submit is increasing. I wake up feeling like this. That's how I know this is going to last. To be honest, I'm glad I went through that hell—that pure hell. God has given me a second chance to make this right. What a HUGE GIFT! I'm getting revelations of how much God loves me. Please pray for me that this rebellious spirit would leave me. I love you so much, Mom.

Sara

So in January of 2016, my husband and I received word that we were allowed to visit Sara at the rehabilitation center. When we arrived, it was on a Sunday morning, and we went to church with her. It was great, lots of Holy Spirit energy! We kept hugging each other, and I gave her a silver eternity ring and a leather Bible with her name engraved on it. She seemed grateful to receive them. On Monday afternoon, we had a meeting with Sara and some of the staff who were taking care of her. I remember her saying that she wanted to control her own life and her money, and her statement was, "Mom, you won't be around forever. I need to make decisions for myself and be self-sufficient."

Thankfully, she was making some progress, improving and gaining skills that she never had before—I was on top of the world! Lastly, a really neat thing occurred when my husband and I were at the hotel while in Pennsylvania—the lights went off in the whole building—except for our room. God certainly was watching over us on that trip. I will never ever forget it as long as I live.

Joy to Despair

Two weeks later, Sara's counselor called me and said that she got kicked out again due to behavior issues, causing a commotion in the dorm. With her one and only bus ticket, she contacted her old friend Danny and went back to Tennessee. (I remember her calling me prior to that and asking for his phone number, and I wondered why). I couldn't believe it! Talk about major disappointment!

Danny called me and said he had picked her up from the bus station. He did not hesitate to tell me that she could not stay with him. She was a totally different person now—and was not comfortable around her anymore. He reluctantly allowed her to stay a week and found a nonprofit organization in Nashville that could possibly help her. The program was very similar to the one in Pennsylvania. It was a six-month program that provided housing, and she could stay there as long as she needed or until she found a job.

At that same time, back home here in Michigan, my friend from church (the gentleman that went with my husband to take Sara to Pennsylvania) called me. He said the Holy Spirit spoke to him and said, "If Sara doesn't adhere to this program, God in His mercy will take her home."

So I prayed, "Abba, I thank you for your faithfulness to Sara, for protecting her and sparing her life so many times. You have always been a good father to her and to me. I am eternally grateful to you and love you and praise you. It's up to her now."

Day One

That Saturday morning, we talked with the nurse. She told us that "Sara was found unconscious on a bathroom floor of a restaurant." Between the EMS and emergency room staff, they performed fifty-three-minutes of CPR. Miraculously, they finally got her heart to start beating again. The first thing I asked was, "What was in her bloodstream?"

Her reply was, "Just her medications that she was prescribed, and also Adderall." I was doubtful that Adderall caused her to collapse, so I asked the nurse if there was a special lab test that could determine what was in her system.

Her reply was, "Unfortunately, the hospital is not equipped for this sophisticated testing." (I did some of my own research and discovered that the Michigan State Police conducts this sort of blood analysis.) It would be three long months before I knew what caused her to lose consciousness.

So Sara's body was on life support, and her brain was showing no signs of normal function. The neurologist stated that a CT scan was performed, and it was turning dark—which meant that it was dying. As tsunami waves of grief were crashing over me, I was agonizing in my head, *What could have caused her to be unresponsive?*

The nurse continued sharing information and told us the name of the restaurant where she was found. We discovered it wasn't far from the hospital. After talking with the manager, she said Sara had come in at about nine o'clock the night before with a young guy, who was wearing a dark cap. She had gone to use the restroom, and he was on his phone, pacing. After about twenty minutes, the manager began to wonder why she was in the bathroom so long. She knocked on the door, but Sara didn't answer.

The manager got another worker and opened the bathroom door. They found my daughter lying facedown on the floor with her pants down.

Together, they pulled up her pants and started performing CPR, and they called 911. She told me there was "drug paraphernalia" near her. The manager had instructed her coworker to "not touch anything." The guy who was with Sara suddenly bolted through the door and fled out into the cold December night. Unfortunately, we never did find out who he was.

In addition, I also made a stop at the local police department. They had taken my daughter's purse and had her car towed to a local impound lot. The officer told me, "Because of situations of this nature, there was nothing they could do to try and catch whoever this guy was. However, he did tell me they found 'crack cocaine' near her, so I assumed that's what she overdosed on."

When we returned home that evening, I wrote in my journal—just as I had been doing for many years.

> Daddy, you know Sara is in the hospital. You know she is on life support and may die. God my Father, I want YOUR WILL TO BE DONE. I don't want Sara struggling and suffering anymore or hurting. I just want her at peace. I want her to be with you. I want her to be enveloped in complete and utter love—your love. She came from you before her conception. I pray she is with you now, and it's okay. I'm okay with it—it will be hard, but I just want you to take her. There is nothing here on this earth for her. No program, no treatment, no person, no doctor, no psychiatrist, no counselor, no pastor or priest that can help her. Only you can help her! God, have mercy on Sara, forgive her sins, and lead her in the way everlasting. Receive her into your heavenly kingdom where there is no pain, no sorrow, no

tears, where no evil can touch her anymore. I release her to your loving care, and I know that someday I will see her again.

As I mentioned before, God does hear and answer our prayers, so be careful what you pray for.

The Mixed-Up Merry-Go-Round

I do not recall how long Sara was in Tennessee at the nonprofit organization. I just remember her calling me and saying she was in trouble—again. She and her roommate did not get along. This girl accused Sara of stealing something from her purse. Needless to say, she got kicked out of that program as well. I felt like I was on this never-ending merry-go-round that would never stop.

As a result of her dismissal from the program, Sara researched Austin, Texas. Once again, we provided her air fare. She had found a boarding house and rented a room. While living there, she met a guy named Sean—of course, he had many issues: drugs and alcohol to name a couple. I believe she was out there for about six months. I found one of her memoirs saying she had to get away from him because he was so messed up.

On the positive side, she temporarily held down two jobs and took the city bus as she had no vehicle. Once again, she called me and said, "It's too expensive for me to live down here. I'm coming back to Michigan." Of course, we flew her back home, and she stayed with us. After two weeks, my husband and I couldn't take it anymore—the disrespectful, spiteful, ornery attitudes had taken over—with vengeance.

We decided to give her an ultimatum—find your own place to live or go back to Texas. She chose Texas. On the way to the airport, she was sitting in the backseat, verbally abusing me. I was fuming inside—but I held my tongue. When we arrived, she got out of the car, and I watched her walk away in the side mirror. I felt a stab of heartache as she disappeared out of sight. I really didn't know if I would ever see her again after that. The last letter I received from her in Texas said, "I'm sorry things will never work out between us. I'm returning the eternity ring." I was no longer mom but Donna.

About a year later, in the spring of 2017, I had heard from some family members that Sara was back from Texas and living in the town she grew up in. I thought, *Oh, no, here we go again.* Later, I found out she lived about five miles away from my house. I don't know how she managed it, but she got her own apartment again and had Puddy with her. I was nervous because I didn't want her coming over and starting trouble with me and my husband. Eventually, she stopped over, and we talked, but I told her things had to change in order for us to build a relationship with each other. We even talked about going to family counseling together.

After everything I had gone through with Sara, this scripture really helped me to not fall apart, Jeremiah 31:3–22. I added her name in this passage to make it more personal for me.

> Long ago, the Lord said to Sara, "I have loved you with an everlasting love. With unfailing love, I have drawn you to myself. I will rebuild you, my virgin Sara. You will be happy again and dance merrily." The Lord has redeemed Sara from those too strong for her. Turn Sara again to you and restore her. For you alone are the Lord Her God. She turned away from you, but then she was sorry. She kicked herself for her stupidity, for she will be thoroughly ashamed of all that she did in her youth. For the Lord will cause something new to happen, Sara will embrace Her God.

If you have never read scripture this way—inserting your loved one's names—I strongly urge you to do it. It is very therapeutic and makes the Bible come alive.

Now, I need to make a pit stop here—"Puddy the cat" was not just any ordinary cat from a barn. Sara, over the years, had developed a strong attachment to her and likened her to a daughter. She had written a letter to God concerning Puddy.

You are an amazing God. You said you are fully invested in me, and you hear my every plea? Well, Jesus, please hear me when I beg you to take care of Puddy's pain. (She is fourteen years old and a diabetic). Please, please, please take it away! I can tell she's suffering, and, Lord, that breaks my heart. God of the universe, take my cat's pain far from her. I can't stand to see her in this state. Please, Lord, have mercy on her and touch her with your healing touch. Please dear God, I beg this of you. I love this cat so much, and I'm so sorry for putting her in the car with me when I was driving crazy. *Please forgive me.* I've been careless with her, but no more. I can't bear to think that I am the cause of her pain. Please fix this whole situation. Let me feel the pain instead of her. I will take her pain. Hear my cry, God. In Jesus Christ's name, amen.

A point I don't want to overlook is that God communicates with me occasionally in dreams. One night, I had a very vivid one. It was about a badger, and it was walking on a path with me. There were people around me, and they were scared, but I wasn't. I picked it up and moved it to the side. It turned to me and said, "Time is short."

I really didn't understand what the dream meant at the time. Later, I looked it up, and it said, the badger represents "past and future." I said, "God, are you preparing me for Sara's death?" I believe God was warning and preparing me for something in the future—little did I know what devastation was coming to completely blindside me.

Living on Borrowed Time

In April of 2018, my daughter overdosed on pills again and was taken to the hospital. Her landlord had found her lying on the bathroom floor banging her head and called 911. When I saw her in the emergency room, I gasped in disbelief. Her head and face were so swollen. I hardly recognized her. In a bizarre voice, I heard her say, "I hate my life, and I know you don't want me in yours." The truth was, it was her unstable behavior I didn't want in my life. I was always apprehensive and disturbed and felt overwhelmed by her decisions and actions. I asked the nurse if the hospital had a chaplain. He said yes and summoned her immediately. I called my Christian coworker, and twenty minutes later, she joined us there—in a room that was becoming oh-so-familiar to me. As we prayed, I clearly remember that whatever drug she had taken was losing its effect on her. No one can convince me otherwise that it was the power of God working on Sara's behalf that night.

Since the hospital had no psychiatric unit, she was transferred to a different facility in another county. She called me every day. We talked again about going to counseling together. It always seemed that when she was in a locked-up situation, we got along better. When she was released, it was near my birthday, which is in early May.

She came to church with me that Sunday and gave me a pretty birthday card. It was a nice change, reading something positive from her. However, on the day of my birthday, she texted me while I was at work. She said she was going to kill herself by drowning. Deep in my heart, I never knew if she was serious or not. I was absolutely frantic and left abruptly and drove over to her apartment. My heart was pounding so hard as I was running through a field in my work clothes.

The street she lived on was in the repaving process, so I had to park a ways from her apartment. When I arrived, I tried talking to her, but she got straight into her car and drove away. Feeling utterly helpless, I called the police, and when they arrived, she pulled into the driveway. The officer talked to her and asked questions, but she acted like everything was fine. He explained to her they had to take her to the hospital. They took her in the police car, and I followed them. While we sat in the waiting room, she would not speak to me. She was mad at me because I had called the authorities. The staff escorted us to a room, and Sara lay there for four hours and did not speak a word to me. This time though, she was not admitted to the psych ward.

I wrote in my journal,

> A lot has been happening again with Sara. She wanted to kill herself again. God, this is clearly manipulation again. This is a vicious continuous pattern with her, so I'm going to back off for a while. I'm so exhausted. I feel like I've been in a war zone. My stress levels were at an all-time high, and I found myself being very short with my husband and the people around me.

After that episode, I went to her apartment to check on her. A guy named Aaron had been hanging around her. I asked where she met him. Her response was the psych hospital from her prior suicidal incident. I said, "Hello," but was suspicious of him. I didn't trust anybody she hung around with. It wasn't long after, she was packing up Puddy and going to his house that was fifty miles away in the city. She told me numerous times, "Mom, I'm moving to the city. I hate this town. There's nothing here for me, no opportunities whatsoever."

As days went by, she was spending more and more time with this guy and would call me and ask "Mom, will you feed Puddy for me? I'm going to Aaron's house for a few days." I found out Aaron had been in jail too and had gotten into trouble with the law. I was just so tired of her hanging around people who were always into some kind of trouble. I thought numerous times, *Is her life always going to be like this, God?*

In June of 2018, Sara called and asked me to take care of Puddy again. She and Aaron were going up North to stay at a very nice cabin in the woods near a lake with his parents. Sara sent me a picture of the cabin on my phone. This cabin was huge and so rustic and pretty. I thought, *She sure has a way of getting around.*

Not too long after, she returned home from up north and had been in the city with Aaron. He had a friend named Daniel who took a liking to Sara. Thankfully, he did not do drugs or get into trouble. He was a good influence on her, and the three of them would hang out together. On one occasion, while they were driving around, she was pulled over for a traffic violation. When the police ran her license, she had a warrant for her arrest. The reason was her negligence. She had failed to appear before the court some years back when she had shoplifted.

We paid her bond, or she would go to jail. I didn't want her to lose her apartment. We found out where she was being held and picked her up. It was so frustrating for us because we did not know the area, and it was dark outside. She told us that there were two warrants on her, both for shoplifting. Therefore, she had to appear before two different judges. I said, "God, please don't let Sara go to jail. She has been getting better, and she finally has her own apartment. I don't want her losing everything that she has worked so hard to gain."

Sara could not afford her own attorney, so she had to have a court-appointed attorney to represent her. She pleaded guilty to the charges. The first judge let her go for the time being, pending the second hearing. However, the second judge was not lenient. Sara had to go to jail. The original sentence was one year. For the chance to have a reduced sentence, she agreed to attend a program, which allowed her to get out earlier. It included church services, which I know helped her to cope with being locked up.

Meanwhile, my husband and I had to decide what to do about Sara's apartment. We paid one month's rent—financially, we could not do more than that. Sara would have to start over again when she got released.

So Puddy came to live with us, and we went to work cleaning out her place. The landlord was very accommodating and kind. I thanked her for being good to Sara. Much to my surprise, she told me Sara was a good tenant and paid her bills when they were due, including her rent.

With all the commotion with her being jailed—in the back of my mind, I was thinking about where was she going to live when she was released. This caused me much anxiety. I didn't see her the whole time she was incarcerated—almost five months—although we did hear from her occasionally. We bought phone minutes for her to contact us if she needed to. Her friend Daniel came to see her frequently and talked to her almost every day. He was so generous putting money in her commissary account to buy things that she needed.

By this time, it was Thanksgiving. My two sons had come over for dinner. Sara called us from jail, and we all had a chance to talk to her. She said, "It's so hard being in jail during the holidays."

I prayed that evening, "God, when she gets out, it's my hope she is determined to get her life on the right path (your path). Holy Spirit, continue to pursue Sara. God, I trust you, and I know you won't let me be disappointed."

Days to Remember

On Monday, December 10, 2018, I got a phone call from Sara while I was at work. She was out of jail and wanted to be picked up. She was so anxious to leave. She had texted me a couple of times, asking if I was on my way yet. I left early from work, and we arrived at 8:30 p.m. It took about four hours to pick up Sara from the time we received her call. When we pulled up to the building, she was standing outside. She was wearing sandals and long scrub pants. When I saw her, I was shocked! She had put on a lot of weight—Sara had always been a small petite person.

Driving home in the darkness, she commented on the pretty Christmas lights that decorated the houses and how good it felt to finally get out of that *hole* as she called it. I remember her saying how nasty the food was. (A Band-Aid was found in the goulash once.) Her days had been spent eating, sleeping, going to church, and participating in a program called Jaws.

When we got home, it was late, and I had to get up for work the next morning. She took her box of stuff from the jail to her room and went looking for Puddy. She was so happy to see her. The hugging began between us. I was relieved that she was home. Once she got settled, I went to bed. At 3:00 a.m., I heard noises coming from the kitchen. It was Sara eating. She said, "Sorry, Mom. I'm just so hungry."

When I got up at 6:00 a.m., she was still awake. (She was too wound up and couldn't sleep.) I made a pot of coffee, and I read my devotional to her before leaving for work. I was hoping she was going to have a good day as my husband was going to take her to run some errands. Her plans were to get her SSI reestablished and get her phone turned back on. As the day progressed, she contacted someone named Brian whom she bought Adderall from.

It really bugged me that was the first thing that she did. She said it gave her energy and helped keep her focused, not to mention it was an appetite suppressant. I know her tremendous weight gain really bothered her, and she was planning to sign up with a fitness program. The following day, we had dinner together and watched TV. She didn't sleep much again that night. The next morning, Wednesday, Puddy and Sara joined me again for morning coffee and reading the devotional. It was refreshing to sit down together and talk about what it said. Her youngest brother, Andrew, had been texting me early that morning, which was unusual. I was reading to her what he was saying that he had a new girlfriend. Sara was giggling because she was happy for him.

Later that day, I texted my husband from work and asked him how things were going with Sara. He replied that she was busy making us some chicken dinner. I smiled because that is something she liked to do—cook. When I got home from work, we all sat together and enjoyed her meal. It tasted delicious—and I really praised her. I could sense she was trying to please us. I was savoring just relaxing with her and talking—spending mom-and-daughter time.

The next afternoon, we decided to go clothes shopping at thrift stores because her clothes did not fit her. She also got a call from her dad—her car was ready to be picked up. Sara had a beater of a car before going to jail. The exhaust was loud, and the dash lights were always lit up. It had been sitting for nearly five months in the parking lot where her dad worked.

I drove into the lot and parked next to her car. Sara went inside the building to get the keys from him. After what seemed like a long time, they came out together, and she sat in the driver's seat. Her dad was checking the tires. I was gazing intently at her facial expressions. It didn't take long to realize she was on the verge of crying. I felt he had said something to upset her. It's like I could read her heart— "Daddy, I love you, but why do you talk to me this way?"

I just wanted to reach out and hold her and protect her at that very moment. I wanted all the hurt to not ever touch her again. After he walked away, she jumped into my car, and I held her and prayed for peace. Afterward, she said, "Mom, I felt the peace as soon as you said it."

I wish she didn't have to see him because she always got emotional. She got into her car and followed me to some other stores. She bought my granddaughter a Christmas present—a My Little Pony horse.

Later that afternoon, back at home, we sat and talked about a lot of things—just the two of us with no one else around. We shared our hearts together and cried and hugged. She said, "Mom, I love you. You did the best you could with what you had." I felt so much relief afterward. That unforgettable time I had with my daughter is tucked away in my heart. A place that is reserved just for her. She even snuggled with me on the couch—I cherish those moments. I could have stayed there forever. (My heart aches as I write this. It's like I'm right there again.) I told her that *I loved her so much*, and she was beautiful.

Without any delay, Sara was able to get a new phone. She was texting people—and this made me very uneasy. I knew from past experience I could not confront her right away. Having her being upset over a presumption would have been reckless on my part. I held my peace—but I thought, *Who in the world is she talking to, and what is she up to?*

As I mentioned earlier, because of Sara's past behavior, there had been some negative feelings in the family, especially with my mother and sister. I wanted the four of us to get together to mend our differences. I was so tired of everyone fighting and quarreling—I just wanted peace and harmony among us. Unfortunately, as much as I wanted this to happen, it didn't.

Finally, it was Friday, December 14, and I had the day off from work. Sara and I got up and had our coffee and devotional together. As she took a shower, I made us some breakfast. My husband and I had some errands to run that morning. Sara had some things she wanted to do. She went shopping at the grocery store and ran into my sister. I was so grateful for that. Later, my sister told me that she seemed nervous, but they talked right there in the store and were hugging. (I wish I could have been there). Sara was so excited that she called me and told me that they ran into each other. I sensed that a weight had been lifted from her, and she seemed to be much happier. I said, "Wow! That was certainly was a divine appointment, wasn't it?"

She cheerfully agreed with me.

When Sara returned home, she showed me everything she bought. We planned on making Christmas cookies, and she was showing me all the festive decorations she bought. She had to get ready to go out for dinner and bowling with her friend Jay. I was really hesitant about her going out with anyone. When she was ready to leave that afternoon, I remember saying to her, "Sara, be home by eleven because we are going to lock the house at that time."

She said, "Okay."

That would be the last time I would ever hear her voice again.

Frozen Memories

My husband and I traveled back and forth to the hospital for several days. That Sunday, Sara's older brother, Marty, came with us to see her. He stood by her bedside. I wanted to give him some time alone with his sister. I went across the hall to a private room and cried. I glanced over and watched him. He was kissing her hand and her forehead, gently caressing her arm and talking softly to her.

When I walked back into the room, he said, "Mom, I felt her lightly squeeze my hand." Maybe she did, maybe she didn't. What he felt at that moment was real to him. (Sadly, the next day, he would be hospitalized from a mental breakdown.) I sat next to her and read out loud Isaiah 43 from the Bible. The only other sound in the room was the life support equipment that was breathing for her. Before I left for the day, I said, "Sara, I love you. I have always loved you and always will."

On Monday, December 17, we arrived at the hospital at 9:30 a.m. I was eager to talk to the neurologist who was overseeing Sara's brain function. My mother, sister, stepdad, and cousin had arrived around the same time. Unfortunately, my mother never got the chance to make amends with Sara. When she saw her, she broke down sobbing, saying, "I'm so sorry, Sara, for you feeling like you weren't loved. We loved you more than you will ever know." I left the room once again so my mother could have time with her first grandchild. Shortly after, my sister and cousin came in, crying and talking to Sara.

Seventy-two hours had passed since they cooled her body. The neurologist came into the room and said there was no change in the swelling of her brain and to call family and friends. Then he said this, "You might want to consider organ donation." My ears heard his voice, and everything around me seemed to stand still. Numbness engulfed me, and I was paralyzed. There was nothing I could do to help her anymore—tragically my only daughter was dying.

In the final analysis—this time was unlike all the other hospitalizations when she was admitted for suicide attempts or drug overdose. She always came back—like a cat that had nine lives. Today, I knew she wasn't coming back.

Later that afternoon, her brother Andrew and her dad came to see her. Andrew shared with me she wasn't there anymore. He knew deep in his heart she was gone. But he was really struggling with letting her go. He felt God saying—"Let her go." He felt the Lord's peaceful presence in the room and felt her fight was over. Andrew held her hand and said, "Sara, you are truly better off being at home than you are here." That was the last time he saw his sister.

Tuesday, December 18, we arrived early at the hospital. I wanted to spend as much time as I could with Sara. I went to her bedside and stroked her beautiful auburn hair, which had grown longer since she was in jail. As I think back, I realized her hair was its natural color that day. Usually, she had some sort of coloring in it. It was so thick and soft. I buried my face in her hair and began weeping as the scent of coconuts filled my nostrils. I thought to myself, *I don't ever want to forget this moment, I want this to be a frozen memory in time.*

Now, I knew I had to call two of Sara's good friends. (They didn't do drugs with her.) I urged them to come and see her as soon as possible. Her good friend, Daniel, had been such a noble and trustworthy person in her life, especially when she was in jail all those months. I thank God for him and the friendship and support he gave to her. I'm forever grateful to him. He arrived and went to her bedside. I stepped out of the room. After his visit, I gave him a bracelet she had made. He started to cry. My heart went out to him, and I gave him a tight hug.

Her other good friend Tami, a good Christian woman, had been there for Sara when she went through some really tormenting times. She confided in me about a time when Sara tried to kill herself by injecting her cat's insulin into her abdomen. Tami rushed her to the hospital. The doctor told her, "If you had not brought her here, she would have died." When Tami visited Sara that evening, she began worshipping and praising God, right there in the hospital room. I'm so thankful for her support and being there for Sara. On the drive home that night, she told me Sara said loudly in her ear, "Let me go."

Meanwhile, the Gift of Life organ donation coordinators were at the hospital that day. I talked to them and answered all their questions regarding Sara's health history to the best of my ability. I told them Sara had nearsighted vision and wore glasses for much of her life. They were very supportive and offered their sincere condolences concerning her.

In order to declare my daughter's death official, two neurologists would have to perform separate brain function tests to see if she would respond. The first doctor started to talk loudly to her, saying, "Sara, can you hear me?" He was nudging her shoulder and shaking it. Nothing happened. I left the room because it made me cry. He checked her pupils, and they were not responding to light. He told me that another neurologist would perform the same test tomorrow.

The next day, Wednesday, December 19, we arrived early again at the hospital. I was informed the second brain function test was performed at 7:30 a.m., and Sara did not respond. At that time, she was declared deceased. I remember feeling—this CANNOT be real.

Shortly thereafter, I had to step out of the ICU. As I was walking through the waiting area, I noticed it was packed with people. I saw a woman crying, and then I started crying again. I went into the washroom, and the Holy Spirit spoke to me, "Go tell that woman who was crying that God loves her, and He wants her to trust in Him."

I said, "Okay, I will."

I went back to the overcrowded waiting lounge and stopped in front of her. I bent down and whispered into her ear, "God loves you, and He wants you to trust Him in your situation."

She looked at me stunned and uttered very slowly, "Okay."

At that moment, I felt God so strongly. I felt this surge of joy and energy flow through my entire being. (It felt like an electrical current went through me.) It was incredible! I remember thinking, *I don't care what anybody thinks. What have I got to lose? I just lost some-one I loved dearly, so what could anybody say or do to me that could be worse?*

Renewed strength and boldness were rising up within me, which I had never experienced before. I knew God was with me and sustaining me each moment. I felt He was carrying me through the worst day of my life even though I was completely heartbroken and crushed. What mother wouldn't feel that? I felt like something was holding me. A friend later told me God infused me with supernatural anesthetic to protect me. Although I was walking through the valley of the shadow of death, I did not fear because I knew God was with me.

That morning—the last day I saw my child—I wrote,

> My heart is broken. Yet I know, Lord, you have been preparing me for many years. Today, I have to make decisions I thought I would never have to make concerning my daughter and what to do with her body. I need to talk to her father about this. I dread it. Help me to be strong through-out this whole day. Despite this awful tragedy, Lord, I want your light and love to shine through me. Help all my family members in their grief. I thank you so much for the precious time I've had with Sara this week. I will play those memories over and over in my mind forever. Now I know how Mary, Jesus's mother, felt when her firstborn son died on that cross. A sword had pierced her heart—mine has been as well. Abba, I love you. I pray you have Sara exactly where she needs to be and that she is finally at peace and rest. I love you, Sara Lynn—until we meet again.

Christmas Day felt very empty to me even when family members were near. My oldest son was in the hospital, and my daughter was dead. Having a Christmas celebration was out of the question. Despite my somber mood, I wrote,

> I praise you, Abba, for your love, your mercy, your provision, and your protection. Jesus, for your willingness to do your Father's will by coming to this earth and showing us what God our Father really looks like. For His goodness and His kindness for His creation. Since December 10, my life has been flipped upside down. The pressure and stress have been monumental, *but God*, through it all, my eyes are on you. Only by your sustaining "grace" and "gentle" hands have I made it through these very dark days. Thank you for holding all of us who are grieving Sara's loss. Abba Father, thank you for Sara's life. Her life was not in vain, for she gave the "GREATEST GIFT" of all HERSELF for the benefit of others, so they would live a long and meaningful life. Your ways are not my ways. Your plans are so much greater than mine. Sometimes we have to lose something of GREAT VALUE in order to gain something much, much bigger than ourselves. So it was with Sara. God, you gave her a greater purpose—something "eternal," something no one could ever take away. Not even the devil. Jesus came to be the ultimate sacrifice for us. Sara died but was destined to be a sacrifice for others that they too would live. I believe that makes her a superhero! Thanks be to God for His sacrificial gift! Luke 18:14, 'For those who exalt themselves will be humbled, and those who humble themselves shall be exalted.' Sara has done just that. Sara, may you hear the words of your Savior. Well done my good and faithful servant.

I would like to share with you how God's goodness and faithfulness have been abundant during these very rough days. It happened at the end of December. A woman our family knows heard my daughter passed away. While praying, she heard God's voice say, "This girl that died, her name is 'Sara.' and she's with me now." Then she heard Sara say, "Don't worry."

I just about lost it! There is NO DOUBT in my mind what she heard was absolutely true, and my Sara WOULD HAVE said something like that!

After Sara's death, the reality was sinking in deeper. Sara was really gone and never coming back. I need to pause and share the last letter I wrote to my daughter:

Dear Beloved Sara,

I'm sorry we didn't get a chance to say goodbye. I'm sorry we didn't have a better relationship. I'm sorry I wasn't more attentive to you when you were growing up. I'm sorry we missed out on enjoying your life and being closer. I'm sorry I didn't have more patience with you. Please forgive me. I know you did the best you could. I know you struggled and lived in torment for many years. It broke my heart more than you could ever imagine. This was not supposed to be this way. I'm not supposed to be burying my only daughter at such a young age. Your life wasn't supposed to turn out this way. I will never forget the first time my eyes saw you—on a computer screen. I will never forget that beautiful image of you, so pure and innocent. I saw your little heart beating. Now thirty-four years later, your heart is beating in someone else's chest. Your lungs are breathing in and out in someone else's body. Your liver and kidneys are functioning too in someone. All because you decided to be an organ donor.

I'm so incredibly proud of you, Sara. I will always be proud of you. I will love you forever into eternity. I pray Jesus will allow us to see one another again someday. Until then, be at peace and rest. I love you so very much.

Mom

I asked God, "I prayed for her countless times. Why did she have to die? Why didn't she come home that night? Why did she go to the city and end up facedown on a bathroom floor?"

Then I heard in my spirit. "She had free will. Death was a result of her choices."

That hit me hard. Sometimes, our free will creates catastrophic results. The ripple effects have a direct impact on other people. When tragedy strikes, the God of comfort will step in and buffer the trauma.

In late winter, I wrote,

God, what the devil meant for evil you have already turned around for good, for my good and your glory and honor. May something grand and wonderful be manifested through this tragedy. May this release a new deeper walk with you, Lord, and an anointing to help other people who have lost someone they love to drugs and mental illness. Abba, I'm looking forward to the longer, warmer days that are approaching, but the truth be told, I miss Sara so much my heart hurts. I never thought I could miss someone so much. Today is a weepy day for me. Get me through this. Please, Lord, restore what the enemy has stolen from me. God, I need your strength and joy. I need your love and comfort today. Holy Spirit, hold my grieving heart. It's so fragile right now. I love you, Jesus, amen.

Friday, December 14, was her "last" conscious day on this earth. The last day she would ever see earthly sunlight or Christmas lights. The last day she would see me and John and her beloved Puddy. The last day she would ever feel the cold of winter on her skin. The last day to listen to her favorite music and to hear the voices of her true friends.

Hence, in March 2019, I received the medical examiner's report. At last, I was going to find out exactly how my daughter died. The results shocked me! A LETHAL DOSE of fentanyl AND acetyl fentanyl. I had to look up what acetyl was because this drug was unfamiliar to me. My findings were very disturbing. Where in the world did this come from? Who in their right mind would ever consider putting these drugs into a needle and giving it to a human being? Someone vile and wicked! I was in total astonishment! I was really struggling with this new information.

I probably will never have the answers to many of my questions. Like, who was the person she contacted to get the drugs? Who was with her when she bought it? Did Sara know fentanyl was the drug given to her? Was she led to believe it was a safe drug to take? Was she duped into taking a different drug than the one she wanted? Why did the guy run away when he knew something was wrong when Sara did not come out of the restroom?

When I read the autopsy report, it said there was a puncture site below her right knee. This puzzled me. Then I remembered she had been complaining about her feet and ankles, how they were hurting when she got out of jail. Then this thought came to me. She didn't want to commit suicide. She must have been in a lot of pain from the increase in her weight. This must be why she injected the fentanyl below her knee where the pain was. Why would anyone give themselves an injection of a pain killer in that spot? That's not the typical place where injections are given. Of course, I cannot be 100 percent sure about how this happened. I have a strong feeling this is what could have taken place on that cold December night. Now, the cocaine the policeman found by her in that bathroom, God only knows where that came from, but that drug was not found to be in her body.

I'm totally convinced that God in His unfathomable mercy said, "Come on, Sara. Enough is enough. Do you want to go back to the chaotic life you've led, or do you want to come home with me?"

Eight months later I would reread my good friend's prophetic statement in my journal, "God in His mercy will take her home." I had completely forgotten about it—I was dumbfounded. God has a plan for everything—even death.

New Beginnings

After days and months of grayness and gloom, I received a large envelope from the Gift of Life. Inside the envelope were communication release forms for me to sign. This would permit me to contact the persons who received my daughter's organs. Also, there was a handwritten letter from the woman who had received Sara's lungs. She shared that she is also a believer in Jesus and expressed a desire to meet me. Throughout my entire life, other than giving birth to my children and accepting Christ as my savior, this letter is a treasure to me. NOTHING CAN COMPARE! I was ECSTATIC! But the most unbelievable thing—this woman's name is SARA! Spelled EXACTLY like my SARA! I was totally blown away! I laughed out loud and yelled, "God, you are so amazing! Only YOU could have done this!"

The next morning, I woke up thinking about Sara A., and it hit me. God is giving me another chance. Not at having a daughter, but to have a relationship with another Sara. God has taken "the ashes" and given them "life" again. I said out loud, "You knew she had to go to jail. You allowed it for a reason. So her lungs would have a chance to heal. They were smoke-free for five months, and now Sara A. has them! Your ways are not even close to our ways. It completely boggles my mind how magnificently you work. I'm so grateful and thankful for your love and faithfulness!"

I'm chuckling as I write this. God has such an amazing sense of humor! Recently, I was having a weepy day, and I asked the Lord for some good news. So guess what arrives in the mailbox? Another envelope from—you guessed it—Gift of Life. Within it was another letter. Unbelievable—but true—a young lady named SARAH received *my Sara's* HEART! Now tell me, what are the chances of two people with that name receiving my daughter's organs? Even though Sara's heart stopped beating for over an hour, it recovered. Now it's pump-ing life once again. If you are not a believer in God, I certainly hope you are considering being one now! I just want to jump out of my skin right now! I will tell you bluntly—this was completely orches-trated by divine, supernatural intervention. I do not believe in coin-cidences. There is not one person who could ever convince me that God is not real. He has been actively involved in my life even when I wasn't aware of it. I assure you, He is active in your life. You just have to look for Him. The Bible says, if you seek Him with your whole heart, you *will* find him. Why? Because *He loves you* and has a great master plan for your life. It's so astonishing!

So now, may I announce, we now have a SARAH 3! Praise to you, my God! Thank you for Sarah's life. Thank you for rescuing her from the "jaws of death" and giving her a "new heart." I pray, Father, if Sarah does not know you, I ask that this "new heart" would lead her to you, right into your loving, gentle arms. Whether she realizes this or not, your hand is upon her, and you desire a relationship with her, today and forever.

Unless a seed falls into the earth and dies, it does nothing. But if it's buried and dies, it grows and produces new life. My Sara had to die to produce a new life for complete strangers. "Abba, you totally amaze me! Death was not final with my Sara. It produced wonderful "new beginnings!"

God, I know you were speaking to me this morning before my feet even hit the floor. "I did it for you. I arranged for Sara and Sarah to receive your daughter's lungs and heart. I did this to help "lessen the blow" of Sara's death so you can know everything you went through all those painful years with her was not in vain."

How incredibly speechless I am at this moment. Sara and Sarah are my rewards on this earth. I am so humbled. My mind cannot wrap itself around this kind of love. The Almighty Creator of the worlds is concerned about me. He knows every tear, every silent ache in my heart. He hears words I cannot express. He knows my inner-most being.

Up to the present time, my dreams from the Lord had become less frequent—but I had a strange dream in April. It was about a woman I never met. She wore thin wire-rimmed glasses and had short salt-and-pepper-colored hair. I gave her a hug and said, "Take it one day at a time." I was bewildered because I didn't know anyone who looked like this person.

The Gift of Life had finally coordinated a meeting with Sara A. and myself. We met in Ohio for the first time on Thursday, September 26, 2019, nine months after my Sara passed away. I told my husband about my dream the morning we left for Cleveland. I thought, *Okay, God, I'm going to see if you were the one that gave me that dream about Sara, my daughter's lung recipient.* The drive took about four and a half hours one way. I was so excited to meet this woman with whom I already felt such a strong connection.

When my husband and I arrived, we met with the coordinator. I displayed some of my daughter's paintings and drawings in the reception lounge. Thankfully, we had a video camera set up to record our meeting. When Sara arrived, she hugged me and cried and said, "Thank you." I was smiling because she was the woman I had dreamed about five months prior. I was eager to tell her about this dream. I happily said, "God has done it again."

As we hugged, I didn't want to let go of her. I had waited with anticipation, nine long months, for this very special day. I gave her two special gifts. The first was a hardcover book that contained pictures of my Sara. The other present was a cross necklace with two pieces of jewelry that personally belonged to her. We had a wonderful two hours and forty-five minutes together. I think I talked the poor woman's ears off. I had so much to tell her about my Sara's life and the events that happened up to the day she died.

I think she was shocked when I told her that my Sara had been a smoker for seventeen years. The day we met was one of the best days of my life. I am so thankful to God for orchestrating all of this. The incredible miracle of Sara A.'s double lung transplant was made possible because my daughter was an organ donor. She and I are now able to contact each other as much as we want to. I'm looking forward to developing a relationship with her—what an amazing gift she is to me!

In the future, I may share this organ transplant story with my local social media. I hope it will show people how very important it is to be an organ donor. I pray it will change hearts and lives by demonstrating God's sovereignty. It was His "divine intervention" that all this took place the way it did. God multiplies life, and through the culmination of events that many times made no sense to me, He was working behind the scenes. Instead of three people dying—only one did.

After our meeting, Sara emailed me her story. It included a blog that her local media had written. The journey of her transplant experience is beautiful. It points directly to the one who made every last detail possible—GOD!

She had shared in her story that she only had two weeks to a month to live. It was certain she would not have lived past the Christmas holiday of 2018. While she was in the hospital waiting for a donor, in the middle of the night, her transplant coordinator came to her room. He explained to her they had high-risk lungs available. This meant in the future, the lungs could be a potential problem for her. Knowing she had a very short time, she agreed to accept my daughter's lungs. It took nine hours for the surgeon to perform the double lung transplant. Her first thoughts when she woke up from the surgery were, *These are not my lungs*, and *I can breathe!*

Oh, how I would have loved to be there to witness that resurrection of life—seeing with my own eyes death being defeated! It was like the devil got a black eye that glorious day! Now this woman has a bright healthy future to look forward to.

As our meeting came to a close, we hugged again and promised to keep in touch with each other. I looked back, and she blew me a kiss—I did the same.

Time Passages

Thanksgiving 2019 has come and gone. I think about my Sara every day. My thoughts drift back to one year ago when she called from the place that was her temporary home—jail. I still recall our conversation—the sadness in her voice echoed, "Mom, it's so hard being here today—Thanksgiving Day." Even now, this causes my heart to be heavy. That was the last holiday her brothers would be able to talk to her—three weeks later, she would be gone.

The holidays are becoming less meaningful now. The decorations and the glitz and glitter are all dimming. All I think of are days gone by when my children were young and innocent, untainted by the world. I'm grateful I cannot see the future because our family would have been prisoners in their own home. I would never have let my babies out of my sight. I view this as protection from God. He knows if we could see the future, we would be unable to live in the present.

I must confess that in the midst of this somber celebration, I began to think about what I'm thankful for. In an instant, my mind gravitated to Sara A. It was important she knew that God had divinely blessed me with her friendship, and she is a true miracle. We have a bond no one can ever separate. I decided to call her and express my gratitude for having her in my life. Her response was, "Thank you. I appreciate that very much." No matter how down I felt about losing my daughter, I will always have this special lady to remind me about how blessed I really am.

For Christmas, I received a beautiful card from Sara A. She wrote, "I know that this holiday season will be a very difficult one for you. Please know that you and your family are in my thoughts and prayers." Her kindness and prayers are what will carry me through this glum holiday. She also sent me a beautiful angel in honor of my Sara's memory. We all have blessings all around us and need to keep our eyes open.

On a melancholy day for me in January 2020, I was thinking about my Sara and missing her immensely. My cell phone rang, and it was Sara A. Immediately, my mood lifted. She asked me how I was doing, and if there were any difficulties getting through the holidays.

I said, "I thought about my Sara the whole time. Christmas really wasn't joyful for me again this year." I asked her how her holiday went.

Her chipper reply was, "It was fantastic. I went all out."

It made my sad heart glad just knowing that this woman nearly died a year ago had a wonderful Christmas with her family and friends.

She said to me, "Donna, I know Sara's death was an accident. If someone really wanted to commit suicide, they would not go to a public restroom and do away with themselves."

Her words confirmed what I already had settled in my heart many months before. I knew my Sara did not want to die. The tears welled up again in my eyes, and my heart ached to hold my child once again.

On a warm summer day in July of 2020, I received a letter from Gift of Life. Enclosed was a handwritten letter and pictures of Sarah, my daughter's heart recipient. Blinking back tears, I gazed at the photos of a young woman who is alive because my daughter's heart is beating inside her.

The day after Christmas in 2020, I received another Gift of Life envelope. I rushed to open it. There was a letter from Sarah. As I'm reading her words, one word caught my breath—*organs*. She is one of only a few people who have had triple transplants. I couldn't believe it! Sarah not only has my Sara's heart but also her kidneys and her liver! I'm stunned, to say the least! I cannot wait to see this miracle woman, who is alive because of a rare triple organ transplant. I never knew such a procedure ever existed. Sarah was sharing with me her family's adventures this past year with pictures and how she is grateful for my Sara's organs. Someday soon, I pray, I will get to meet her and her family.

Meanwhile, I have to share something very dear and near to my heart. Our beloved Puddy, my daughter's cat, passed away five days after Christmas. My husband and I took her to the vet because she had been losing weight and wasn't eating. In my gut, I knew her time with us was coming to an end. She was almost seventeen years old. After hearing the vet say there was nothing more we could do for Puddy, we made the heart-wrenching decision to put her to sleep. I knew she was suffering, and I just couldn't stand the thought of her being so sick. It felt like I lost Sara all over again. The agonizing pain of losing something I love is hitting me hard. I pray that they are together in heaven and will never have to be separated again.

It is now July 2021. It has been two and a half years since my Sara went to heaven. Our world has been experiencing a worldwide pandemic—COVID-19. Life in general was at a standstill. The mandates affected the economy, our jobs, and our health. My hopes of meeting Sarah were diminishing. I didn't want to lose contact with this miracle girl. I have such an intense desire to see her.

Friday, July 9, 2021, my phone rang while I was at work. I ignored the call because I was not supposed to be on my phone while working. The phone rang again. I glanced at the number, and I had a feeling that the call is important and that I really needed to answer it. I picked up my phone and said hello. A male voice said, "Hello, Donna."

My gut told me this is the call I've been waiting for—it's Sarah's father.

He continued, "I've wanted to call you so many times, but I didn't know what to say. So you are writing a book!"

I replied, "Yes, I am."

Then I heard Sarah's mother in the background. She asked me if I had any other children.

I replied, "Yes, two sons and a granddaughter." They were both talking to me at the same time on speakerphone, and then Sarah joined the conversation. It was WONDERFUL to hear her voice! As our discussion progressed, her mother asked me if I heard of her daughter's organ transplant on social media.

"No, I had not heard anything about it," I replied. To my astonishment, Sarah's triple transplant made national and worldwide news! I was awestruck! My Sara's organs made medical history! It was performed at the University of Chicago where the history-making of the "double triple" that took place on December 21, 2018.

Sarah McPharlin is the seventeenth person in the United States to receive this type of rare procedure. I'm still reeling from this mind-blowing news. God has done it again!

In October of 2021, my phone rang again at work; but this time, I knew who was calling—Sarah's father. He had wonderful news for me. I was FINALLY going to meet Sarah!

One week later on a gloomy rainy Friday, Sarah and her parents arrived. I had been waiting nearly three years. We talked and shared for three hours, and I got to hear my daughter's heart beating in her chest! I gave her some of my Sara's trinkets in a little wooden box. As our time together came to an end, they promised to come back and spend more time with me and my husband. I'm so thankful for what God has done in Sarah's life. She is a determined young woman who has a strong fighting spirit. I'm blessed to have her and her family in my life.

Now my journey is complete in the written sense. *But God* is still writing HIS STORY in the life of Sara A. and Sarah McPharlin. Their astonishing stories of love, faith, courage, and hope will be echoing through the pages of time and into eternity.

True life accounts can be so intriguing and arouse curiosity in people. It's our human nature. Stories that start out tragically but have a happy silver lining ending and give us much-needed hope. Maybe you cannot always see it with your eyes, but you just know beyond a shadow of a doubt that God was involved, and it cannot be fully explained.

To see the news footage that touched millions of people on this amazing story, go to—youtube CBS this morning triple organ transplant—click on the video with the title that reads; 2 patients who forged a friendship undergo rare triple transplants at same hospital, and also http://www.chicagomag.com/chicagomagazine/ September-2019/ the double triple transplant

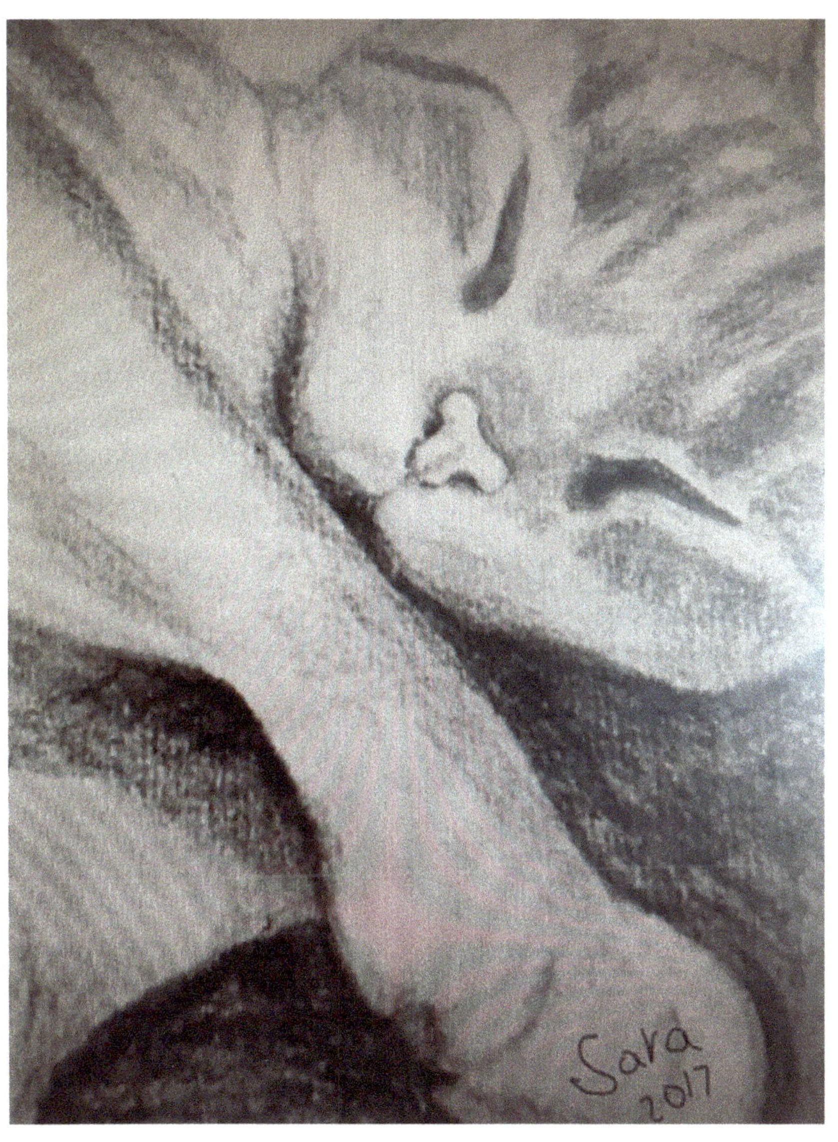
Sara
2017

Sara really loved
her niece

Mom and Daughter

A Note from the Author

It is my hope that when you read these words, your eyes will be opened and that you would know the one true God—the Creator of heaven and earth, the one who died to forgive you of every sin and knows everything that you face today. He sees the bigger picture. He looks ahead to all your tomorrows. He never stops working behind the scenes on your behalf. Why? Because He is crazy in love with you. The God of pure love wants you—a relationship with you that will last forever.

Ask Him into your heart and life to forgive you of all your wrongdoings. Believe in Him and His endless love for you personally and what He did for all humanity so you will never be separated from Him so that where He is, there you may be also. May God bless you!

Additional Note

The cover picture of this book symbolizes how God took the ashes of my daughter's life—and sprang forth beauty—three lilies that represent three Saras and how two lives are changed forever.

A Note from Donna's Best Friend, Tina

Sara was an outgoing beautiful young lady. I remember the first time I met her—she had a dazzling smile and piercing blue eyes. But underneath lies uncontrollable mental sickness. I remember countless times praying with her mother, Donna, for the well-being and safety of her wayward troubled daughter. I will never forget the excruciating pain and heartbreak I could see in her eyes and hear in her voice. Many times her mother would set aside her agenda to work tirelessly to seek help for Sara. Several attempts were made, but they were not successful. It was so devastating to watch my friend in all her relentless love and effort, trying everything in her power to help her daughter. She never stopped trying and praying—even until Sara's last moments. Sara is free now and in the arms of Jesus. Words cannot express the amazing depth of a mother's love—this is something only God can provide within us.

My sister wrote this on Facebook about Sara.

> I've never, in my entire life, felt so empty and sad at Christmas time. The merry is gone. I know this holiday will never be the same as they once were. There will always be a void that will be impossible to fill. I'm never going to see my LuLu again. It just isn't fair! The mere thought of getting old and gray, while she remains forever young, is a cruel reality our family is forced to face. The years will go by, and she will still be thirty-four years old—a vibrant red-haired beauty, as she has always been. I can hardly wrap my head around this. It almost makes me feel crazy mad! But then, I am comforted by the thought in knowing it had to be more than just coincidence that we ran into each other at the grocery store last Friday morning—the same day this tragedy struck. As soon as she came through those glass doors, she immediately spotted me and called out with the slightest hint of hesitation in her voice. Our eyes met and smiles emerged. Shamefully, my mindset was *Gee, I didn't brush my teeth or comb my hair today,* as I had just gotten out of work. I had not seen my niece in at least three years. Time, distance, and circumstances created this invisible wedge between us. Bonds were broken, and trust was lost. Life happened, mistakes were made. And

yet amongst all that hurt and absence, we still hugged, talked some, then hugged some more. We forgave each other and explained our hearts. She confided that she was getting her life back on track, but she seemed nervous as if she was really trying to prove something to me—something she wasn't sure of herself. Looking back, it makes me sad—incredibly sad. She didn't need to prove anything to me. After a few more minutes of small talk, we hugged one last time, a great big bear hug—the kind that lifts you off your feet. Little did I know, it would be the last time I would see her pretty, soft freckled face. I still manage to smile and thank God for that final moment that was shared only between us. It's a memory so special; it will be impossible to forget—locked away deep within me. I realize it was a gift—a Christmas gift. I can honestly say it is the best gift I have ever received. I love you, Sara. May you find peace, love, and joy. Until we meet again…

About the Author

Donna gives all the credit to God in writing this book. She says, "I'm not a writer, but He is." Never in her wildest dreams did she ever think it possible to write a book. "I'm just an ordinary person, who was in desperate situations and sought His help—and He showed up—in my dreams. He will do the same for anybody—if they just ask and believe."

Donna lives in Michigan, with her husband, John, near the beautiful shores of Lake Huron.